KU-702-964

Football's
FUNNIEST
JOKES

Jim Chumley

summersdale

FOOTBALL'S FUNNIEST JOKES

Illustrations by Robert Duncan

Summersdale Publishers Ltd
46 West Street
Chichester
West Sussex
PO19 1RP
UK

www.summersdale.com

Printed and bound by Tien Wah Press

ISBN: 978-1-84024-745-9

Substantial discounts on bulk quantities of Summersdale books are available to corporations, professional associations and other organisations. For details telephone Summersdale Publishers on (+44-1243-771107), fax (+44-1243-786300) or email (nicky@summersdale.com).

Football's
FUNNIEST
JOKES

Jim Chumley

Editor's Note

They say football is 'the beautiful game' but, as this book shows, it's a funny old one too. Here we have scoured the football pitches, terraces and commentators' boxes across the land to bring you the best jokes the game can offer. This arsenal of gags, guffaws and giggles will ensure you're never caught foot-in-mouth or score a social own goal again.

Telling jokes is a bit like playing football; you need to think on your feet, stay on the ball, hammer it in at an unexpected angle and know when to stop dribbling. It doesn't matter whether you support the Red Devils or Wanderers, Spurs or Gunners; kit yourself out with this book and you'll never let the side down for laughs.

Turf War

What happens after England
win the World Cup?

The manager turns off
the PlayStation.

'Sheffield Wednesday couldn't hit a cow's arse with a banjo.'

DAVE BASSETT

'If Everton were playing
down at the bottom
of my garden, I'd
draw the curtains.'

BILL SHANKLY

'Where shall we take the team on holiday this year?' asked the Everton captain's wife.

'Let's go to Bath,' replied the captain.

'Bath!' cried his wife. 'Why there?'

'They have open-topped buses,' replied the captain. 'The team never usually have the opportunity to go on one.'

Which cartoon character
supports Celtic?

Yogi Bear – he always manages
to outsmart the rangers.

Ashley Cole goes into a
bar and says, 'Just a half
for me, then I'll be off.'

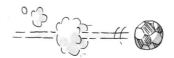

What's the difference between Accrington Stanley and a pencil?

At least the pencil has one point.

Manager's Box

The manager described his new signing as a wonder player.

'Why do you call him that?' asked a journalist.

'Because,' replied the manager sadly, 'whenever I see him play I wonder why I signed him.'

Two boys were caught scrambling over the turnstiles last Saturday at Wigan. They were given a severe warning and dragged back to watch the second half.

Reporter: Can you take free kicks with both feet?

Striker: No one could do that – if they were kicking with both feet, what would they stand on?

'The easiest team for a
manager to pick is the
Hindsight Eleven.'

CRAIG BROWN

'You've come last of twenty teams in the league!' shouted the manager.

'Well, it could have been far worse,' sighed the goalkeeper.

'How on earth could it have been worse?' screamed the manager.

'Well, there could have been thirty teams,' replied the goalkeeper.

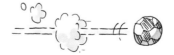

Chairman: That was a pretty dismal game today.

Manager: Well, the crowd were behind me all the way.

Chairman: Were they?

Manager: Well, most of the way. I ducked down an alley and lost them before they could catch me.

'This is the deal,' said the manager. '£80,000 a month now, £100,000 a month in two years.'

'Great,' replied the midfielder. 'I'll see you in two years, then.'

'I can't believe I didn't score that penalty,' cursed the striker. 'I could kick myself.'

'I doubt it,' sniggered the opposition manager.

'Even Ferguson and Wenger had their recurrent weaknesses; neither, to take a common instance, appeared capable of distinguishing a top-class goalkeeper from a cheese and tomato sandwich.'

PATRICK BARCLAY

Striking Gold

The manager rings his striker
and asks, 'Where are you?'

'I'm in my garden,'
replies the striker.

'Did you know there's a match
on today?' shouts the manager.

'Yes,' says the striker. 'But you
said it was a home game!'

A local team in Ancient Greece were three-nil up when the away manager called for a substitution. Their striker came off the pitch and on trotted a horse with the torso and head of a man, to gasps from the crowd.

'Oh no, they're bound to score now,' groaned the home captain. 'They've brought on their centaur forward.'

Why did the footballer
buy Clearasil?

Because of his penalty spots.

'David Batty is quite prolific,
isn't he? He scores one goal a
season, regular as clockwork.'

KENNY DALGLISH

How do you tell the difference
between Emile Heskey
and Ikea furniture?

The furniture is *supposed* to
be in pieces in the box.

'Dad,' said the striker's son, 'can you finish my maths homework while I go and play football?'

'I don't think that would be right,' replied the striker.

'I doubt it would,' said his son, 'but at least it'll look like I've tried.'

A Safe Pair of Hands

'The Pope was a soccer goalkeeper in his youth. Even as a young man he tried to stop people from scoring.'

CONAN O'BRIEN

Why are vampires
terrible goalkeepers?

They always run away
from crosses.

'Which position are you
playing this weekend?' asked
Jim. 'Are you in goal again?'

'I think I'll be in defence, actually,'
replied Bob. 'I heard the manager
say I'll be the main drawback.'

Why was the keeper sitting
on the doormat?

He was waiting for the goalpost.

'Our goalkeeper can jump as high as the crossbar,' boasted one captain.

'That's not difficult,' replied the other captain. 'The crossbar can't jump at all.'

Why did the goalkeeper have so much money?

He was a careful saver.

What's the difference between the Sunderland goal and a taxi?

You can only get four in a taxi.

'Poor Scott Carson. Just two more hands and another chest and he would have saved it.'

JIMMY GREAVES ON ONE OF THE GOALS THAT PUT ENGLAND OUT OF EURO 2008

Who was the worst player in the insect football tournament?

The fumble bee.

What do you call a girl standing between two goalposts?

Annette.

Going for the Cup

Why is a successful football
team like a lingerie shop?

It has a full range of cups
and lots of support.

Why are Newcastle like a tea bag?

They don't stay in the cup for long.

'Man offers marriage
to woman with FA Cup
final tickets. Please
send good colour
photograph of tickets.'

What's the difference between the Invisible Man and Fulham?

You're more likely to see the Invisible Man at a cup final.

'I've just named the team I would like to represent Wales in the next World Cup: Brazil.'

BOBBY GOULD

Where do teams keep their trophies?

In the cup drawer.

A team of ants were practising
their free kicks on a saucer.
Afterwards, they retired to
the spoon for a team talk.

'Right then, lads,' said the captain.
'Big game next week – our
first time playing in the cup.'

Taking it for the Team

What did the Scottish captain
say to the referee when he asked
if he had a coin for the toss?

'You can borrow this one, but I'll
need your whistle as a deposit.'

'I've bought a Tottenham roving season ticket,' boasted Derek.

'Well,' replied Alan, 'I've got an InterRail pass. That's far better.'

'How's that?' asked Derek. 'You won't see much football with that.'

'Maybe not,' retorted Alan. 'But at least I'll spend longer than ninety minutes in Europe.'

Which team make more considerate lovers, England or Italy?

England; who else can be on top for nearly ninety minutes and then come second?

How do you save a Manchester United supporter from drowning?

Take your foot off his head.

Why are West Brom like a
piece of chewing gum?

They always find themselves
stuck to the bottom of the table.

'My parents always beat me,' sobbed little Johnny.

'Who would you rather live with? Your auntie and uncle?' said the social worker.

'No!' cried Johnny. 'They always beat me as well.'

'Where can he live where he won't get beaten,' asked the social worker to her boss.

'See if there's any space up at Queens Park Rangers,' suggested her boss. 'I don't think they've ever beaten anyone.'

A couple had moved to a hut in the Himalayas to escape from the hustle and bustle of life.

'My football team lost their match today,' said the husband sadly.

'How on earth do you know that?' asked his wife.

'It's a Saturday.'

Why did the football club change its name to You Can't Play for Shit FC?

So it sounded like their fans were cheering them on.

A Portsmouth supporter was being interviewed by a local reporter.

'Who do you blame for the disappointing streak of results?' the reporter asked. 'The defence? The goalkeeper? The strikers? The manager?'

'No,' replied the man. 'I blame my parents.'

'Why's that?' asked the reporter, puzzled.

'Well,' said the man, 'if I hadn't been born in Portsmouth I wouldn't be disappointed, would I?'

A pirate took his parrot to the betting shop. When the football scores were being announced, the parrot looked up and said, 'Bugger it, Sunderland lost again.'

'That's pretty impressive,' exclaimed another man. 'What does he say when Sunderland win?'

'I've no idea,' replied the pirate. 'I've only had him for two years.'

Hallowed Ground

'This place is confusing,' the fan commented of the new stadium.

'Why?' asked his mate.

'Well, you're supposed to sit in the stands,' replied the fan. 'But you're not allowed to stand in the sits.'

'The English football
team – brilliant on
paper, shit on grass.'

ARTHUR SMITH

Why was the pitch so slippery?

Because all the players
dribbled on it.

What did the manager do when
the pitch became flooded?

He sent on his subs.

Why didn't the fans like the new stadium on the moon?

There was no atmosphere.

On the Terraces

How many Grimsby fans do you
need to change a light bulb?

All three of them.

Why are Cardiff fans like piles?

They're a pain in the arse.

What's blue and yellow
and travels at 100 mph?

A Brazilian football fan
falling out of a plane.

The seven dwarves were driving to the Bolton match when they suddenly lost control and swerved down a bank, rolling the car upside down. When the paramedics arrived they feared the worst.

'How many of you are there?' they shouted into the wreckage.

'Seven,' came back the reply. 'We were off to the Bolton game. They're going to win the cup today.'

'Well, thank goodness for that,' said one paramedic. 'At least Dopey's OK.'

'Why do Arsenal fans smell? So the blind can hate them as well.'

JOE LYNHAM

A man took his son to see Stoke City play. He gave the man at the ticket desk £40 and said, 'Two, please.'

'Certainly, sir,' replied the ticket seller. 'Would you prefer midfielders or defenders?'

Why should you never run over
a Liverpool fan on a bike?

It might be your bike he's riding.

'Why do you always book
two seats?' one Millwall
fan asked another.

'One is to sit on to watch the
game,' replied the other, 'and one
is to throw when the riot kicks off.'

'You look glum. What's wrong?'

'My wife's just had a baby.'

'But that's great news!'

'Not really. I've just watched my football team lose 8–0 and now I'll have to make my own supper as well.'

Foul Play

'I used to play football in my youth but then my eyes went bad so I became a referee.'

ERIC MORECAMBE

The local team were playing an Icelandic team who were visiting. Towards the end of the match, the referee called the local players over.

Referee: There'll be ten minutes stoppage time today, lads.

Captain: What? But there haven't been any injuries – just two bookings.

Referee: Yes, but the two people I booked were called Gunnar Heiðar Þorvaldsson and Haraldur Freyr Guðmundsson.

'I never comment on referees and I'm not going to break the habit of a lifetime for that prat.'

RON ATKINSON

What's the technical term for a Scotsman in the World Cup?

Referee.

Striker: **Could you send me off if I said you were the worst referee I've ever known and my granny could do a better job than you?**

Referee: **Yes, I most certainly could.**

Striker: **What if I just thought it but didn't say it?**

Referee: **Well, I couldn't do anything about that.**

Striker: **I'll just leave it at that, then.**

'You can shove that red card where the sun doesn't shine!' screamed the defender at the referee.

'Too late,' replied the referee. 'It's already full of three yellow cards and a corner flag.'

'I need a hobby,' sighed Tom.

'You should join the local football team,' suggested Brian.

'But I don't know anything at all about football,' protested Tom.

'Don't worry,' replied Brian, 'you could referee for them instead.'

Why did the footballer hate his Christmas present?

It had a red card attached to it.

Fever Pitch

'We've run out of salt and pepper in the club restaurant,' cried the head caterer.

'This happens every May,' replied the manager. 'It's the end of the seasoning.'

Why did the monk
take up football?

He wanted to kick the habit.

'Don't worry,' said the footballer,
following an alarmingly
loud belch during a match.
'It was just a freak hic.'

A footballer lent his pencil tin to a friend, who was rooting through it and pulling out protractors and set-squares.

'What's this?' asked the friend, holding up a very complex-looking piece of equipment with lots of angles and lines.

'That's an offside rule,' replied the footballer.

Who brings a rope onto
the pitch at matches?

The team skipper.

'There's only one ship that's never docked at Liverpool,' explained the dock worker to the tourists.

'Which is that?' asked one tourist.

'The Premiership.'

The defender was clouted
in the head during a tackle
and knocked out cold. As the
paramedic waved a towel at him
and sprayed water on his face
to revive him, he came round.

'Bloody hell,' he exclaimed. 'It was
sunny when I fell over; this wind
and rain's come from nowhere.'

'Can Timothy come down to the park for our game this evening?' asked Michael.

'No, he hasn't finished his homework yet,' replied his father.

'Well, can his ball come down to the park?' said Michael.

Have you enjoyed this book? If so, why not write a review on your favourite website? Thanks very much for buying this Summersdale book.

www.summersdale.com